Y0-BDF-354

WHY?

A Book of Reasons

Irving and Ruth Adler

The John Day Company — New York

 Published by The John Day Company, 62 West 45th Street, New York 36, N.Y., and on the same day in Canada by Longmans Green & Company, Toronto.

Library of Congress Catalogue Card Number: 61-13113

Manufactured in the United States of America

This a book of riddles. But these riddles are not jokes. They are questions about the everyday things around you. You cannot find the answers to these riddles by guessing. You can find the answers by looking at things carefully and thinking about what you see.

First try to find the answer to each of the riddles yourself. Then look up the answer in this book to see if you have found the reason why.

Why does a dog's tongue hang out when the dog is hot?

On a very hot day a dog pants just as you do when you have been running. He keeps his mouth open and his tongue hangs out. *Saliva* (sa-LIE-va), or spit, drips from his tongue. Here is the reason why.

Dogs, like people, are *warm-blooded* animals. Their body temperature is always the same, even on very hot or very cold days. There is something inside the body of every warm-blooded animal that keeps the temperature the same. *Sweat glands* (swet) in your skin help do this for you. On a hot summer day you sweat a lot. The sweat makes your skin wet. The water in the sweat dries up. As it dries up, it pulls heat out of your skin. In this way your sweat helps to keep you cool.

But a dog has almost no sweat glands. He cools off in another way. When he is hot, a lot of saliva is made by glands in his mouth. The saliva makes his tongue wet. He keeps his mouth open and his wet tongue hangs out. When the saliva on his tongue dries, it pulls heat out of his tongue. This helps keep him cool. He also pants or breathes fast. His panting makes the saliva dry faster and cool him off faster. There is so much saliva in his mouth that some of it drips from his tongue.

Why are snakes easy to catch on a cool day?

A snake likes to bask in the sun on a cool day. It will find a flat rock and coil up on it. If you come upon the snake, it will not wriggle away. You can catch it easily. Here is the reason why.

A snake is a *cold-blooded* animal. Its body temperature is not always the same. On a warm day, its body is warm. On a cool day, its body is cool. When its body is cool, the snake cannot move quickly. It cannot wriggle away quickly and hide in the tall grass or under a rock. So a snake is easy to catch on a cool day.

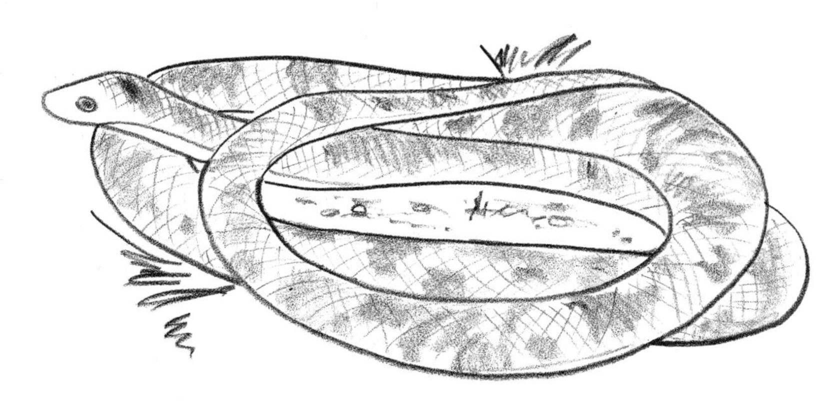

Why does a cat's hair stand up on a cold day?

When a cat is out on a cold day, its hair sticks up straight all over. Its tail looks like a wire brush. Here is the reason why.

A cat is a warm-blooded animal. The cat's thick fur coat helps keep it warm in the wintertime. The fur coat is made up of many hairs that grow out of the cat's skin. The hairs trap air next to the cat's skin. The trapped air keeps heat from leaving the cat's body. So it makes the fur coat warm. The fur coat can be made warmer if more air is trapped next to the cat's skin. This happens when it is very cold. Cold makes the skin pull tight around the hairs. When the skin pulls tight, the hairs stand straight up. When the hairs stand straight up, more air is trapped.

When a cat is afraid, its skin pulls tight, too. So, when a cat is afraid, its hairs stand straight up.

When the hairs lie flat, not much air is trapped

When the hairs stand up, more air is trapped

Why do you get "goose-pimples" when you are cold?

Have you ever gone swimming when the air was very cold? Afterward your arms and legs were covered with millions of tiny little bumps, or "goose-pimples." Here is the reason why.

You are a warm-blooded animal, just like a cat or a dog. You don't have a fur coat to keep you warm. Little hairs grow out of your skin. But they are not close enough together to trap air, so they don't keep you warm. That is why you have to wear clothing.

Even though you don't have a coat of fur, your skin acts as if you do. When your skin gets very cold, it tightens around the little hairs. The tight skin around the little hairs looks like a pimple. The tight skin makes the hair stand straight up.

When you are afraid, your skin pulls tight around the little hairs, too. So you also get goose-pimples, when you are afraid.

Each ring stands for a year

Why do tree rings tell you the age of a tree?

In the Museum of Natural History in New York City there is a round piece of the trunk of a redwood tree. This tree was very large and very old when it was cut down. You can tell that it is very large by measuring it. It measures 25 feet across. You also can tell that the tree was very old when it was cut down. You can do this by counting the number of rings you see in the piece of trunk. Here is the reason why.

Redwood trees grow in the mountains of California. They grow in a place that is not hot all year round. It is also not cold there all year round. Trees that grow in places like this don't grow all year round. They start growing in the springtime, when the ground gets warm. They stop growing late in the summer. They start growing again the next spring. When they start growing in the springtime, a layer of wood grows just inside the bark of the tree. This is the spring wood. The layer of wood under the bark in late summer is the summer wood. The summer wood doesn't look the same as the spring wood. So it is easy to tell when the tree began to grow each spring. It is also easy to tell when the tree stopped growing in the late summer. The spring layer and the summer layer make a ring. Each ring stands for a year in the life of the tree. By counting the rings, you can tell how long the tree was alive.

Why can a fly walk on the ceiling?

A housefly walks right side up the way people do. It can walk uphill and downhill. But it can also do some things that people cannot do. It can climb up a slippery glass wall and it can walk upside down on the ceiling. Here is the reason why.

A housefly can do these things because of the kind of legs it has. Like all insects, it has six legs. Each of its six legs has a little foot. Each little foot has claws and sticky pads on it. These grip the glass wall or the ceiling, so the fly doesn't fall off.

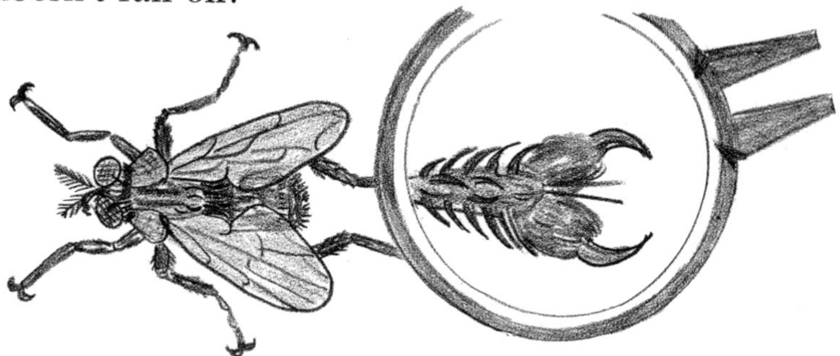

Fly

Foot with claws and sticky pads

Why are the Eskimoes of the Far North broad and short? Why are the Negroes of hottest Africa tall and narrow?

People live all over the world. There are tall people and short people. There are fat people and thin people. There are people with broad frames and people with narrow frames. There is no best way to be. What is best depends on where you live. The Eskimoes who live in the Far North are broad and short, because they live where it is cold. The Negroes of hottest Africa are tall and narrow because they live where it is hot. Here is the reason why.

People are warm-blooded animals. The food they eat is burned in their bodies. This makes the heat that keeps their bodies warm. It is very cold where the Eskimo lives. His body keeps losing heat all the time through his skin. He can live in the Far North only if he can keep warm. The furs he wears help keep him warm. The meat and fat he eats help keep him warm. And the shape of his body helps keep him warm, too. A broad short body has less *surface* (SIR-fess) than a tall, narrow body. There is less skin through which to lose heat. So the broad, short frame of the Eskimo is best for people who live where it is very cold.

A person can live where it is very hot only if his body can lose a lot of heat through his skin. He can lose a lot of heat through his skin if he is tall and narrow. A tall, narrow frame has more surface than a broad, short one. Then there is more skin through which to lose heat. So the tall, narrow frame of the Negro of hottest Africa is best for people who live there.

Negro of hottest Africa and Eskimo

Why can't you see well when you come indoors on a bright, sunny day?

When you come indoors, out of the bright sunlight, everything looks very dark. You can hardly see. You have to put out your hands to keep from bumping into things. In a little while, you can see clearly again. Here is the reason why.

There is a little opening in the front of your eye that lets light in. The opening is called the *pupil.* It is the black in the middle of the colored part of your eye.

You can see things if light comes from them. The pupil lets light from the things you look at come into your eye. Inside the eye, the light shines on a part of the eye called the *retina* (RET-in-a). The picture of what you see is made on the retina.

Suppose you are outside on a bright sunny day. In the bright sunshine, a lot of light comes from the things you look at. Then a lot of light shines on the retina of your eye. So the retina of your eye gets used to a lot of light.

Then you go indoors. Here the light is weak. Not much light comes from the things you look at. So not much light shines on the retina of your eye.

You have just come indoors, from the bright sunshine. So your eyes are still used to getting a lot of light. It takes some time for the retinas to get used to getting less light. So it takes some time before you can see things that don't have much light coming from them. That is why everything looks dark at first.

In about half a minute, your eyes get used to the weak indoor light. Then you can see things that are indoors very well.

Your eyes keep getting used to the weak light more and more. After a while, you can even see very dark things. That is why you can even see things at night, when there are no lights on.

Why don't the fish freeze when ponds freeze over?

In the wintertime it is very cold. Often it is so cold that water freezes. Then ice covers the ponds. Sometimes it is so cold that even the rivers freeze over. Why don't the fish that live in the water freeze, too? Here is the reason why.

When water in a pond freezes, it freezes from the top down. The air above the pond is very cold in the wintertime. The cold air makes the water at the top of the pond get very cold. When water gets colder, it gets heavier. The heavier water sinks to the bottom of the pond. The colder water is then at the bottom of the pond. Meanwhile, the water in the pond keeps getting colder and colder. The colder, heavier water keeps sinking to the bottom of the pond.

This keeps on, until just before the water freezes. Then the coldest water *stops* getting heavier. It begins to get *lighter*. Water that is almost frozen doesn't sink to the bottom of the pond. It floats on the top instead. Then the coldest water is at the top of the pond. So, when the water cools still more and begins to freeze, the water at the top of the pond freezes first.

The water that freezes at the top of the pond makes a cover of ice over the pond. There is pond water under this cover of ice. Fish can live in this water even though it is very cold.

If the air stays very cold for a long time, this cover of ice gets thicker and thicker. Sometimes it gets so thick that the pond freezes all the way to the bottom. When this happens, many of the fish in the pond freeze and die. This hardly ever happens.

Why do some things float in water and other things sink?

Fill a pan with water. Now hold a stone just below the surface of the water. Then let go. The stone sinks to the bottom of the pan right away. Here is the reason why.

The stone takes up space. When the stone is under the water, it has pushed some water out of place. The water tries to push back into its old place. So the water pushes up against the stone. Meanwhile, the weight of the stone makes the stone push down on the water. But the stone weighs *more* than the water it has pushed away. So the stone pushes down on the water harder than the water pushes up against the stone. The *stronger push down* makes the stone *sink*.

Now hold a cork just below the surface of the water, and let go. The cork pops up to the top of the water and floats. Here is the reason why.

The water pushes up harder than the cork pushes down. So the cork floats.

The cork takes up space. When the cork is under the water, it has pushed some water out of place. The water tries to push back into its old place. So the water pushes up against the cork. Meanwhile, the weight of the cork makes the cork push down on the water. But the cork weighs *less* than the water it has pushed away. So the water pushes up against the cork harder than the cork pushes down on the water. The *stronger push up* makes the cork rise and *float.*

Here is the rule for things that float in water and things that sink in water:

When something is under water, if it is heavier than the water it has pushed out of place, it sinks.

When something is under water, if it is lighter than the water it has pushed out of place, it floats.

The stone pushes down harder than the water pushes up. So the stone sinks.

Why can a boat made of steel float in water?

A solid steel ball sinks in water like a stone. But a boat made of steel floats like a cork. Here is the reason why.

A boat takes up a lot of space. Much of the space in a boat is filled with air. There is air in its cabins. There is air in its engine rooms. There is air in its holds, even when they are filled with goods. Air is much lighter than water. So the boat, with everything in it, is lighter than water. That is why the boat floats.

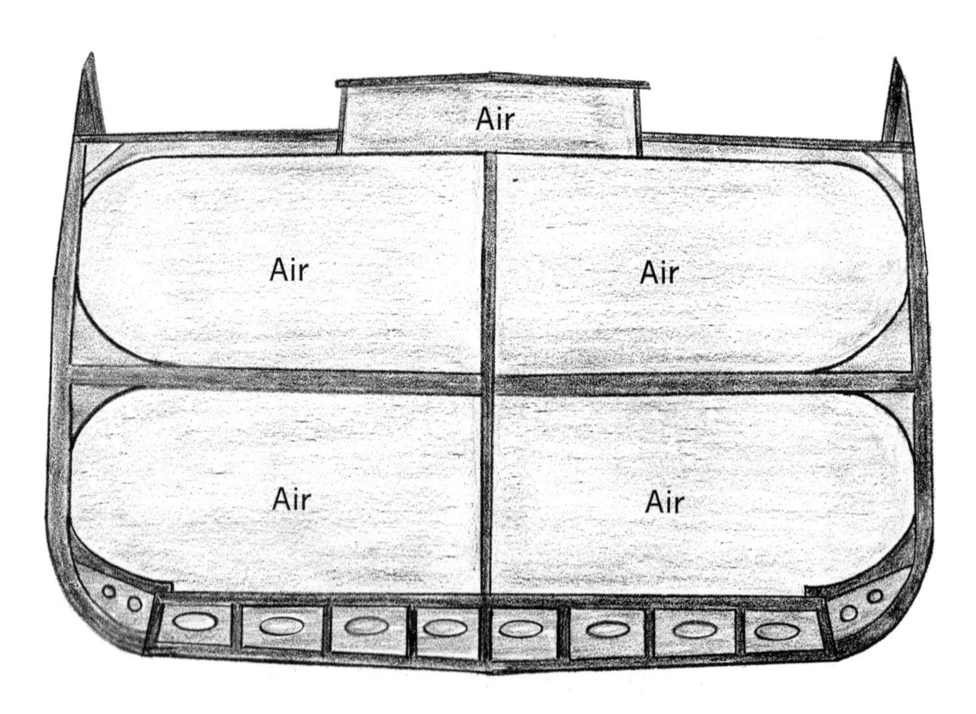

Much of the space in the boat is filled with air

Why can a gas balloon sail off into the air?

Have you ever had a toy gas balloon? It tugs hard at its string. If you let go, the balloon sails off into the air. Here is the reason why.

The air around you has many gases in it. It is mostly *oxygen* (OX-i-jen) and *nitrogen* (NY-tro-jen). *Hydrogen* (HY-dro-jen) and *helium* (HEE-lee-um) are gases, too. They are lighter than oxygen and nitrogen. So they are called lighter-than-air gases.

When a balloon is blown up, it pushes aside some air. A gas balloon is filled with hydrogen or helium. A gas balloon weighs less than the air it pushes aside. So a gas balloon floats up in the air, just as a cork floats up in water.

Hydrogen gas is lighter than helium gas. A balloon filled with hydrogen will float higher than a balloon filled with helium. But balloons filled with helium are safer than balloons filled with hydrogen. Hydrogen burns easily, but helium does not burn.

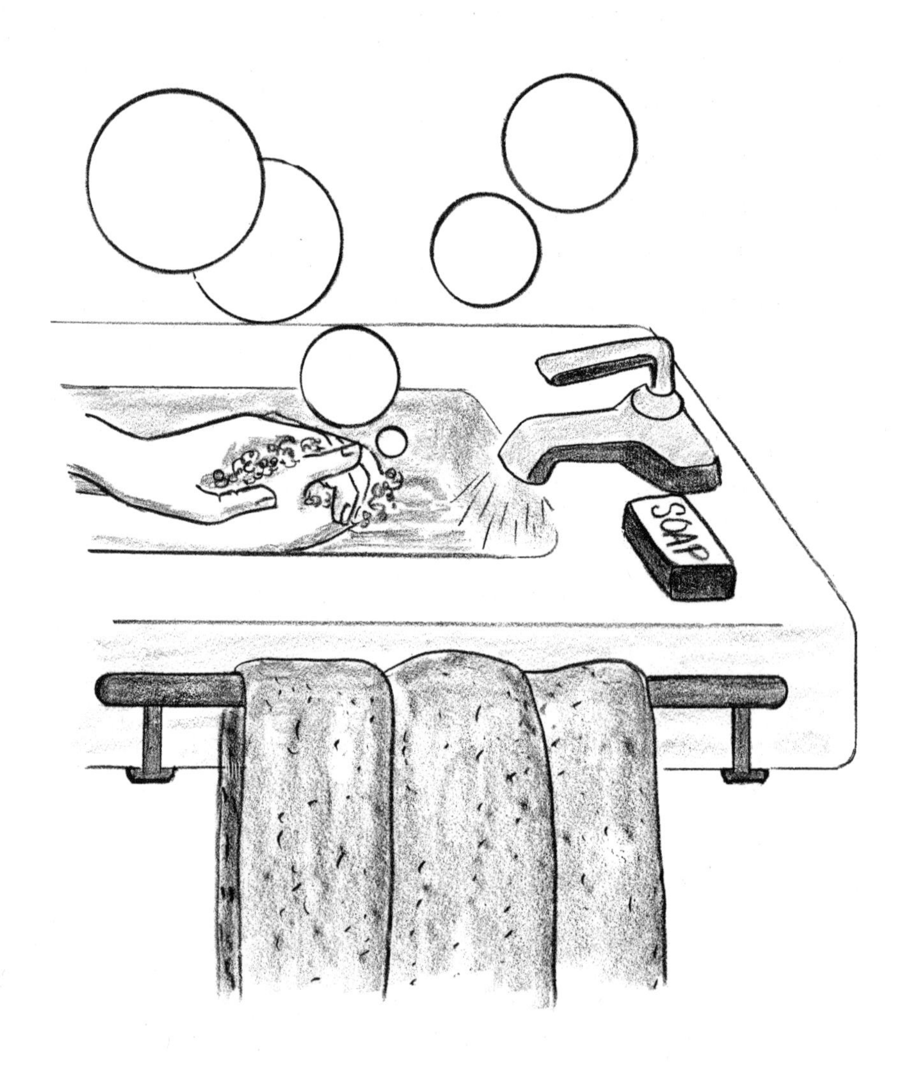

Sticky Molecules

You wash your hands several times a day. You dry your hands with a paper towel or a towel made of cotton. Why does the towel make your hands dry?

To find the reason why, you will have to learn some facts about how *liquids* (LICK-wids) behave. After you have learned these facts, you will then be able to answer many other questions, too. You will know why raindrops and soap bubbles are round, and why some insects can walk on water. You will know why you wet your hair to keep it in place. You will also know why salt is put on icy sidewalks and roads in the wintertime.

* * * * * *

Everything in the world is made up of *molecules* (MOLL-eh-kules). The tiniest bit of air is a molecule of air. The tiniest bit of water is a molecule of water. The tiniest bit of salt is a molecule of salt. Molecules are so tiny that one molecule by itself cannot be seen. Even so, molecules have been weighed and measured. If fifty million molecules of air were put in a row, they would take up only half an inch!

When molecules are close enough, they pull on each other. When molecules pull on each other, this pull makes them stick together. In a drop of water there are many molecules of water that are stuck together. All of the molecules in the drop are of the same kind.

Sometimes molecules of different kinds stick to each other, too.

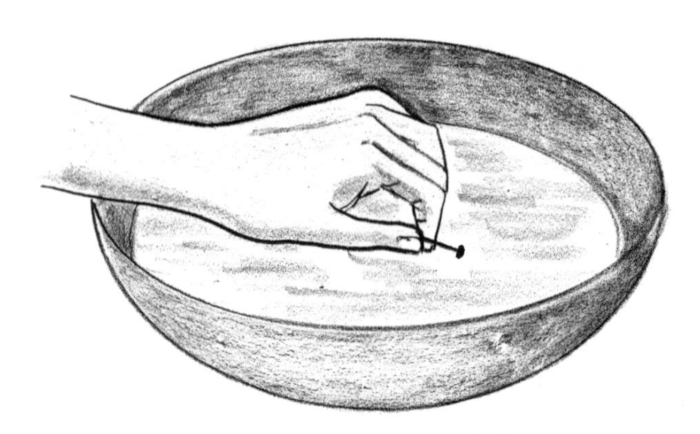

The pin floats on top of the water

Why can a steel pin float on water?

Fill a bowl with water. Then take a straight pin that is perfectly dry. Hold the pin level and carefully lay it down on top of the water. Even though the pin is made of steel, it will float on the surface of the water. Here is the reason why.

The water is made up of millions of molecules. There are molecules at the surface of the water, where the water touches the air. There are more molecules of water underneath the surface. And there are molecules of water which touch the bowl.

The molecules of water which touch the bowl, stick to the bowl. The molecules of water at the surface of the water stick to each other. They also stick to the molecules of water under them. So the surface of the water is like a thin skin. It acts as if it were fastened to the bowl and pulled tight. If something pushes down on a tight skin, the skin stretches. But the skin tries to stay as small as it can. It tries to keep from stretching. So it pushes back.

The pin pushes down on the water in the bowl. It makes a dent in the surface of the water. This makes the surface bigger. But the surface of the water is like a stretched skin. It tries to get as small as it can. So it pushes up against the pin. The pin is very light. The surface of the water pushes up against the pin just as hard as the pin pushes down. So the pin floats on top of the water.

The *water strider* (STRY-der) is an insect that can walk on the surface of water. It has a little body and long, bent legs. Its feet look like straight pins. Because the water strider is so light, its feet stay on top of the water just the way a pin does.

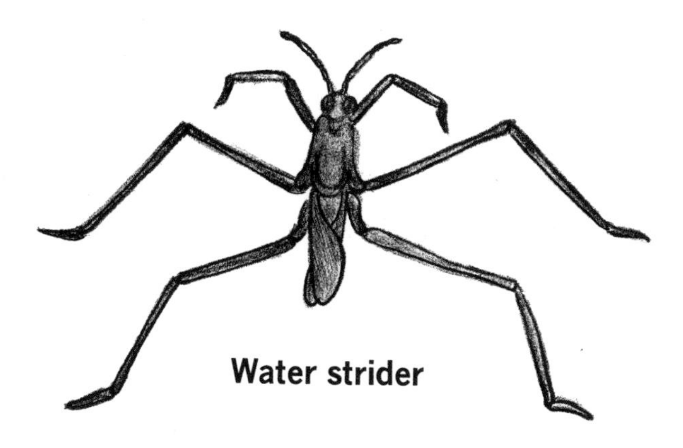

Water strider

Why is a raindrop round?

You can make drops that are like raindrops with a medicine dropper. Fill the glass tube of the dropper with water. If you color the water with some ink it will be easier to see. Slowly press the rubber bulb at the end of the dropper. A bit of water is pushed out at the open end of the dropper. This tiny bit of water looks at first like a little cup. Here is the reason why.

The molecules of water at the surface of this bit pull on each other. They are also pulled by the molecules that are just above them, inside the bit of water. Because of these pulls, the surface of this bit tries to get as small as it can. It is smallest when it is round at the bottom, like a cup.

Keep pressing on the rubber bulb. More and more water is pushed out of the dropper. This water makes the little cup larger. The weight of the cup begins to pull it away from the dropper.

Meanwhile, the surface of the little cup still tries to be as small as it can. The cup begins to look more and more like a little ball. A thin neck of water holds it to the tip of the dropper. At last the neck becomes so thin that the little ball breaks off and drops. It is almost round, but the pull of its own weight makes it look like a pear. So each drop that falls from a medicine dropper is pear-shaped. Raindrops are almost round, too.

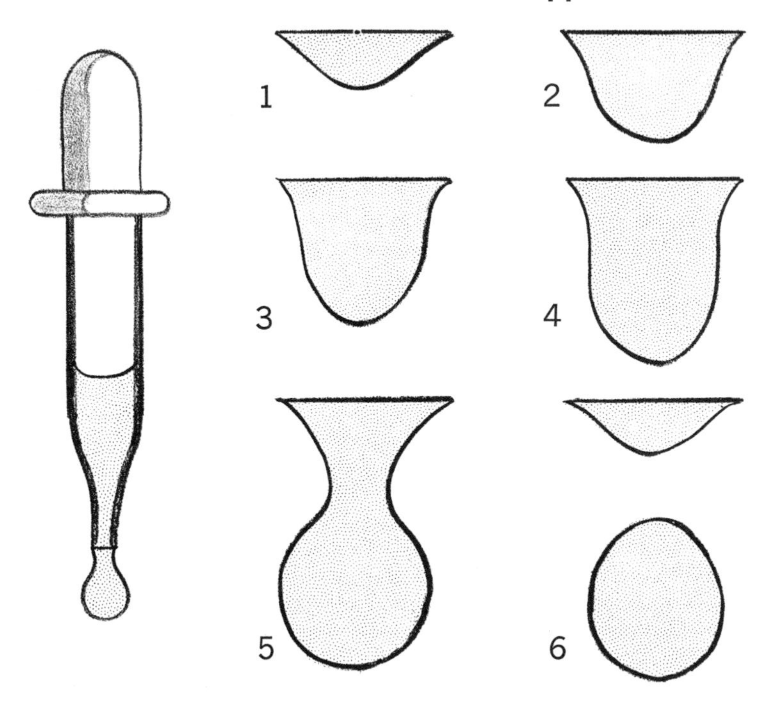

Why is a soap bubble round?

A soap bubble is made by trapping some air in a thin skin of soapy water. The skin acts like a rubber balloon. Because the skin tries to get as small as it can, it pushes in against the air. So the soap bubble becomes round, just as a drop of water does. The bubble is so light that its weight does not pull it out of shape. So a soap bubble is a perfect ball.

Why do you wet your hair to keep it in place?

You can keep your hair in place by making it wet. Here is the reason why.

When you wet your hair, there is water around each hair. The surface of the water around each hair tries to get as small as it can. So there is a little tube of water around each hair. If two wet hairs are brought close enough, the water tubes around them touch. The surface of the two tubes of water tries to get as small as it can. To make the surface smaller, the two tubes come together to make one tube. Now one tube of water is around the two hairs. So it holds them together.

When a lot of hair is wet, all the little tubes of water come together to make a skin of water. The skin of water is like a rubber cap, holding your hair in place.

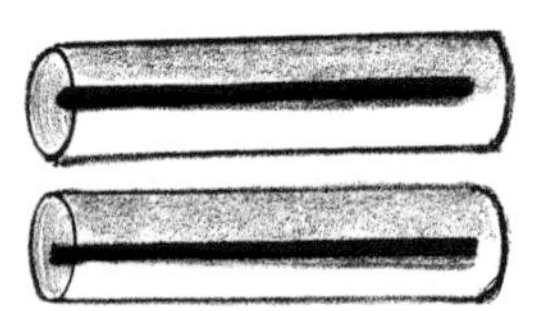

When you wet your hair, there is a little tube of water around each hair

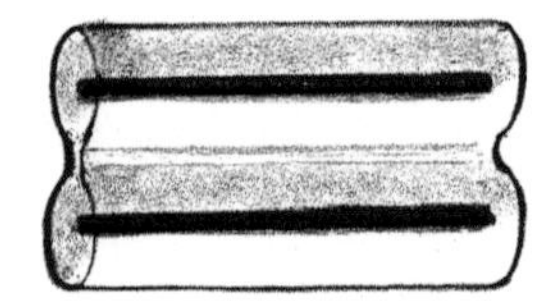

If two wet hairs are close enough, the water tubes around them touch

The two tubes make one tube around the two hairs, holding them together

Why doesn't your wet hair stay in place when you swim underwater?

When you swim underwater without a cap, your hair looks as if a strong wind is blowing it about. Here is the reason why.

If you swim underwater without a bathing cap, there is water everywhere around your head. So there are no little tubes of water around each hair. There is no skin of water to hold your hair in place. So your hair does not stick together. It spreads out in the water. It looks the way it does on a windy day.

The water bends up where it touches the glass

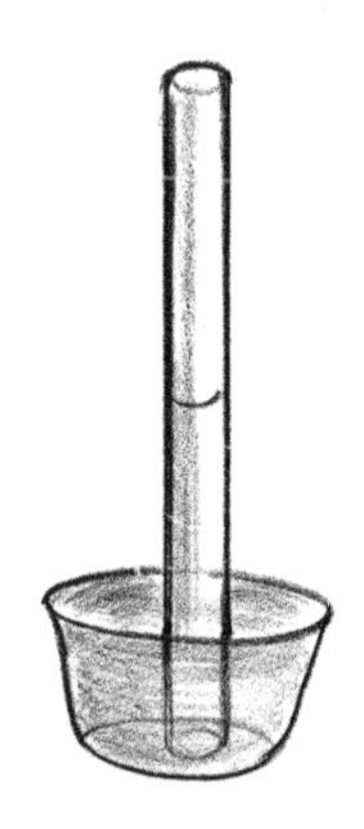

The water climbs up the tube

Why does a towel make you dry?

This is the question that was asked on page 20. Now at last you can find the reason why.

Molecules of water stick to molecules of glass more than they stick to other molecules of water. So we say that water *wets* glass. You can see this easily if you pour some water into a glass. The surface of the water, where it touches the glass, is not straight. It bends up toward the glass.

Now put one end of a very thin glass tube into a dish of water. The water wets the glass so the water sticks to the inside of the tube. The surface of the water bends up near the tube. But the surface of the water inside the tube is like a skin of rubber. It tries to get as small as it can. So the water that sticks to the sides of the tube pulls the water up the middle of the tube. In this way the water slowly climbs up the tube. Meanwhile, the weight of the water in the tube tries to pull the water down. When this pull down is as strong as the pull up, the water stops climbing.

The surface of a cotton towel is made up of thousands of tiny loops. The air spaces between the loops are like little tubes. Water can wet cotton, just as it wets glass. So the water on your wet hands creeps up these little tubes when you wipe your hands with a cotton towel.

The surface of a paper towel is rough. There are many little air spaces in it. So a paper towel acts like a cotton towel. That is why a paper towel can dry your hands, too.

A blotter also has a rough surface with many little air spaces. Ink climbs into these air spaces in the same way that water climbs into the air spaces of a paper towel.

The roots of plants look like thin hairs. They are really very thin tubes. Water from the ground climbs up them in the same way that water climbs up a glass tube.

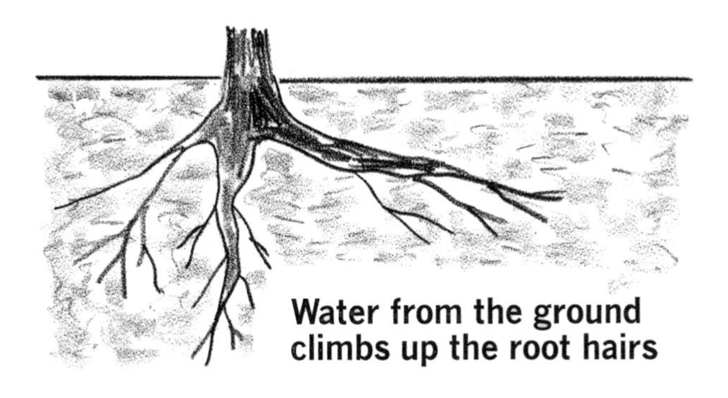

Water from the ground climbs up the root hairs

Why is salt put on icy sidewalks and roads in the wintertime?

Sometimes it rains in the wintertime. Rain water covers the sidewalks and roads. Suddenly it may get very cold. Then the water on the sidewalks and roads freezes. Ice covers them now. It is easy to slip on the ice and get hurt. So salt is put on the icy sidewalks and roads. It makes them safe. Here is the reason why.

Salt, like everything else in the world, is made up of molecules. Water molecules stick easily to salt molecules. Water and salt mix to make salt water.

It must be very cold for water to freeze. It must be

Salt is put on icy sidewalks

even colder for salt water to freeze. Often it may be cold enough for water to turn to ice. But it may not be cold enough for salt water to turn to salt ice. So the salt water stays as water.

When salt is put on an icy sidewalk or road, water molecules in the ice stick to the salt molecules. So each bit of salt has water molecules all around it. The salt mixes with the water molecules that stick to it. Often it is not cold enough for the salt and water to stay frozen as salt ice. Instead, the salt ice melts and becomes salt water. So the sidewalks and roads are safe now because they aren't covered with slippery ice any more.

Why is salt put on dirt roads in the summertime?

A dirt road gets very dusty when there hasn't been any rain for a long time. Cars go over the road and make the dust fly. The dust bothers people who live near the road. So they put a layer of salt on the dusty road. Here is the reason why.

There are some water molecules in the air. The molecules of water in the air stick easily to the molecules of salt on the road. This makes the road wet.

When a dirt road is wet, many small bits of dust are joined together by the drops of water. This makes large lumps of dust. The lumps are too heavy to fly in the air when a car goes by.

Why shouldn't you leave a towel with one end in a sink full of water and the other end hanging over the side of the sink?

If you were ever unlucky enough to do this, you know what happened. After a while, you found a large puddle of water on the floor under the sink. Here is the reason why.

The air spaces between the loops of the towel act like many little tubes. The water in the sink wets the towel, and begins to climb up into these air spaces. Soon the water reaches the part of the towel that rests on the edge of the sink. Then it crawls into the part of the towel that hangs over the side of the sink. The weight of the water pulls the water down through this part of the towel. The towel gets wetter and wetter as more water crawls into the air spaces. Finally the towel can't hold any more water. Then the water begins to drip onto the floor.

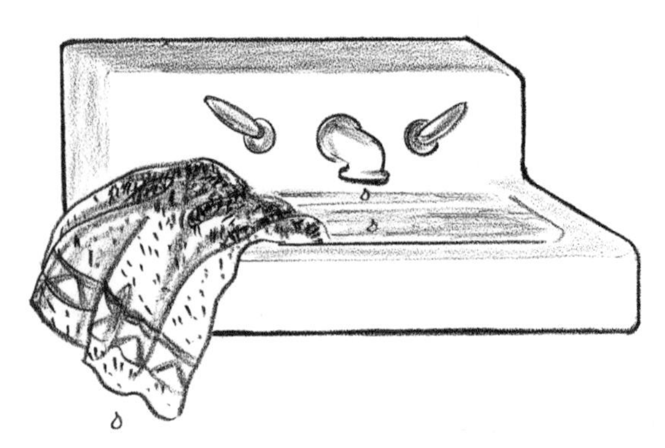

The water begins to drip onto the floor

A long time ago people used kerosene lamps to make light. The dripping towel helps you see how one of them works. A kerosene lamp has a piece of cotton called a wick that dips into a bowl of kerosene. The kerosene climbs up the air spaces in the wick. When the lamp is lit, the flame burns the kerosene as fast as the kerosene climbs up the wick. When the flame is out and the lamp isn't being used, the wick is turned all the way down inside the bowl. Then the kerosene inside the wick won't drip over the side of the bowl.

Ordinary candles work in the same way. A candle is made of paraffin (PAR-a-fin) with a cotton wick inside. When a candle is lit, a little bit of the paraffin at the top of the candle melts. The melted paraffin climbs up the wick and burns together with the wick. As the candle burns, more paraffin melts and climbs up the wick. So the candle gets shorter and shorter. Melted paraffin keeps the wick burning until all the paraffin is used up.

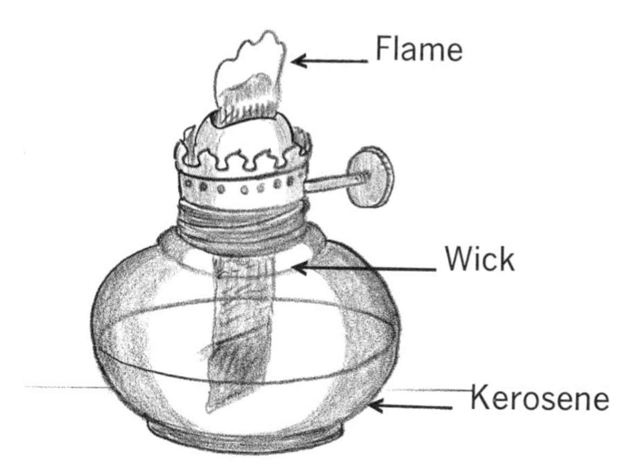

The kerosene climbs up the wick

Why are powders sticky?

A lady powders her face to make herself prettier. She knows that the powder will stick to her skin and will make it look smooth. Here is the reason why.

Face powder is made from a very soft mineral called *talc*. A lump of talc, like everything else in the world, is made up of sticky molecules. The molecules inside the lump use their stickiness to hold the talc together. The molecules on the surface of the lump of talc are also sticky. The stickiness of these surface or outside molecules makes them stick to other things. But a lump of talc won't stick to something else. There just isn't enough outside stickiness. Why, then, does a powder of talc stick?

Break a lump of talc into two pieces. Some talc that had been inside the lump is now on new surfaces made by the break. So some inside molecules have become outside molecules. As you break the talc into many pieces, more and more inside molecules become outside molecules. When there are more outside molecules, there is more outside stickiness. If talc is crushed into a powder, the bits of talc have so much outside stickiness that they stick easily to other things.

Why does a pencil write?

Pencils used for writing or drawing are usually called lead pencils. But the black stuff that writes is really not lead at all. It is made from another very soft mineral called *graphite* (GRAF-ite). Graphite is so soft that little bits of it break off when it is rubbed.

When you write with a pencil, the paper rubs the graphite in the pencil. So little bits of graphite are rubbed off. These little bits make a fine powder. A graphite powder is sticky for the same reason that a face powder is sticky. The stickiness of the graphite powder makes it stick to the paper. The graphite powder that sticks to the paper is the writing on the paper.

The graphite powder that sticks to the paper is the writing on the paper

Why do clothes get dirty?

Sitting on the floor makes your clothes dirty. Working in the garden makes your clothes dirty. Shoveling coal also makes your clothes dirty. Here is the reason why.

Dust is made up of little pieces of many things. Dust floats around in the air and finally settles on the ground. Bits of dust, because they are so tiny, are very sticky. So, when you sit on the floor, the bits of dust stick to your clothes and make them dirty.

The earth in which you plant your garden is usually lumpy. When you dig the earth, the earth breaks up into many little pieces. These tiny bits of earth are very sticky. So, when you work in the garden, they stick to your clothes, making them dirty.

Coal is in the same family as graphite. When you shovel coal, tiny bits of coal break off from the lumps of coal and float around in the air. These tiny bits of coal are very sticky. When they fall on your clothes they stick to them, making them dirty.

Clothes are made dirty, then, by things that break up easily into little pieces to make a fine powder. These tiny bits are very sticky. When they touch your clothes, they stick to them.

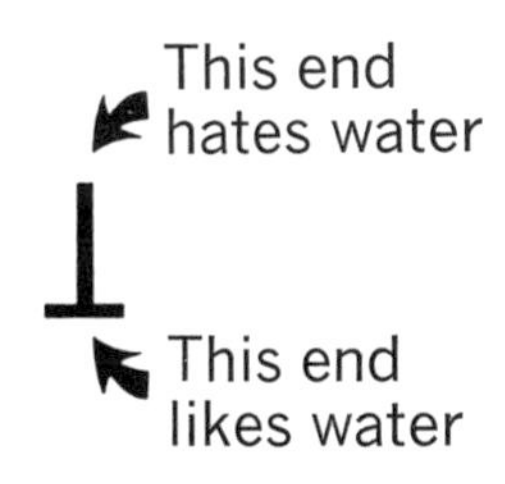

Each molecule of soap has two ends

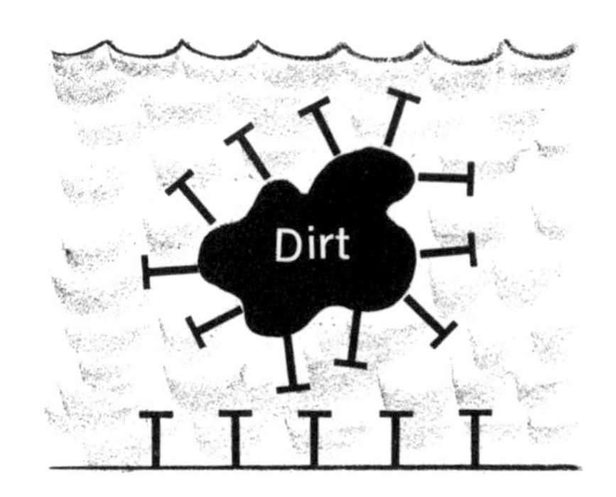

Each bit of dirt is tied to the water by soap molecules

Why does soap make clothes clean?

Soap cleans clothes because soap likes water and hates water at the same time. Each molecule of soap has two ends. One end of the molecule likes water. The other end of the molecule hates water.

When dirty clothes are put into soapy water, the molecules of soap place themselves in a special way. The end of the molecule that hates water sticks to the dirt. So each bit of dirt has molecules of soap all around it. In this way the dirt on the clothes is loosened by the soap. A washing machine shakes the clothes that are in it. This helps the soap loosen the dirt faster.

Each molecule of soap also has an end that likes water. This end sticks to a water molecule nearby. So each bit of dirt is tied to the water by soap molecules. When the clothes are rinsed, the water carries the dirt away.

Why do jets leave trails in the sky?

On a clear day, you may see long white trails high up in the sky. They are made by jet planes. Here is the reason why.

Let's first look at a teakettle boiling on the kitchen stove. You can tell when the water in the kettle starts to boil. You can see a cloud coming out of the spout of the kettle. Perhaps you think this is a cloud of steam. If you do, you are wrong. Take a more careful look at the boiling kettle. You can see that the cloud doesn't touch the spout at all. There is a space between the spout and the cloud. Steam, coming out of the kettle, is in this space. The steam cannot be seen. The cloud that you see is made of tiny drops of water.

The water in the kettle is made up of molecules. The molecules are moving all the time. If they are heated, they move faster. If they are cooled, they move more slowly. When the water in the kettle is heated, the water molecules move faster and faster. As they move around, they push in every direction. They even push against the surface of the water. When the water has become very hot, the molecules push so hard that they pop right out of the water into the air. The molecules that pop out of the water are no longer a liquid. They are a gas, like air. Water molecules that are a gas are called *steam* or *water vapor* (VAY-per).

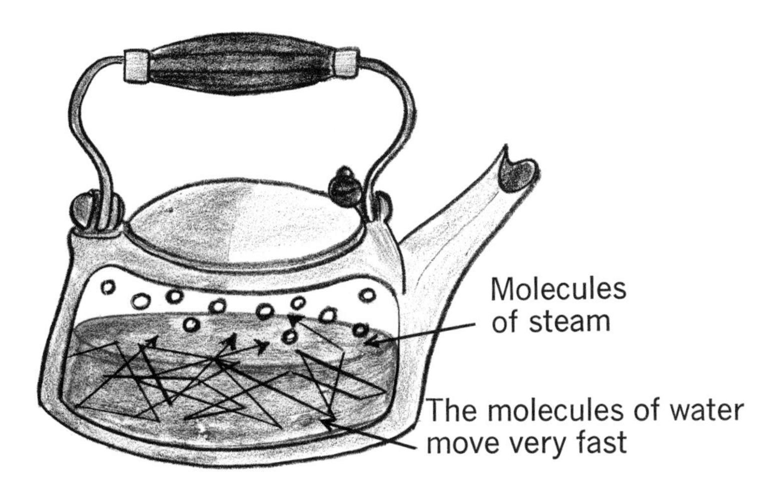

When the water becomes very hot, the molecules pop out of the water as steam

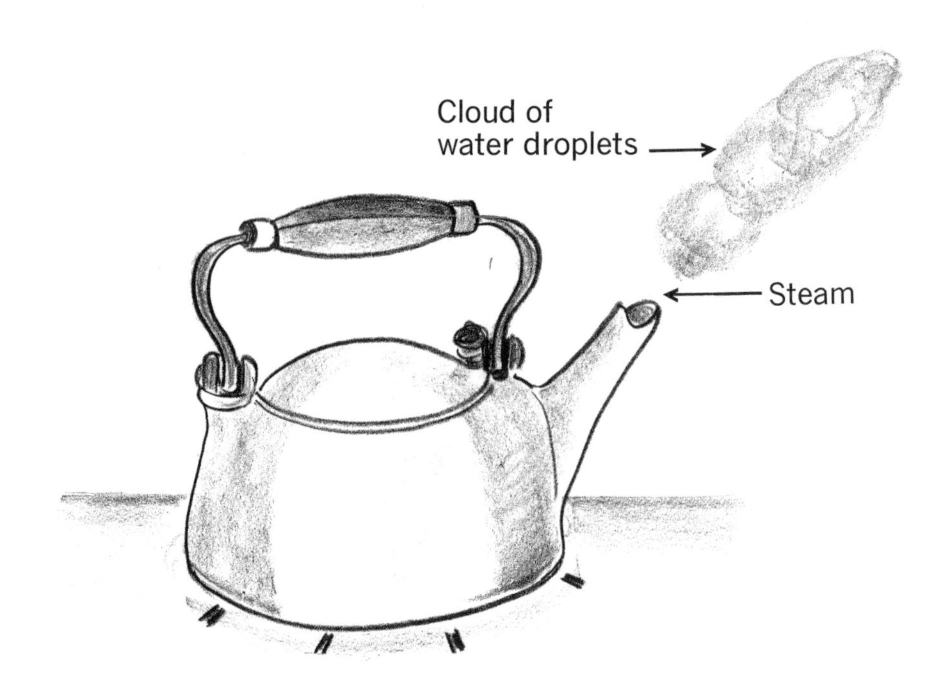

As soon as the steam leaves the kettle, it is in the cooler air of the room. Because the room is cooler, the molecules of steam slow down. When they slow down, they change back to water again. The molecules of steam change into tiny drops of water. These drops make the white cloud you see coming from the spout of the kettle.

Jets fly many miles above the earth. The air high above the earth is very cold. The gases that come out of the jet and push it forward are very hot. There is steam in the jet gases. As soon as the steam leaves the jet, it is cooled by the air. It is cooled so much that it forms tiny pieces of ice instead of drops of water. These bits of ice are called ice *crystals* (KRIS-tals). The jet trails you see on a clear day are made of ice crystals.

Why do windows become frosted in the wintertime?

Blow on a window pane and whisper "Hah" very loudly. You will see a cloudy circle on the window pane. This has happened because there is water vapor in your warm breath. As soon as the water vapor strikes the window, it cools and changes to tiny drops of water. The cloudy circle on the window pane is made up of little drops of water.

Sometimes, when you get up in the morning in the wintertime, you will find frosty pictures on your window panes. This happens when it is very cold outside. Air is everywhere inside your house. The air touches the window pane. The air has water vapor in it. The coldness outside makes the window pane very cold. The cold window pane cools the water vapor that touches it. It cools the vapor so much, that it is changed into ice crystals. The frosty pictures that you see are made of ice crystals.

Frosty pictures on the windows

Why does it take longer to boil an egg at the top of Pikes Peak than in New York City?

A ranger and his family live near the top of Pikes Peak. Housekeeping is never easy for people who live far away from towns. For this family, even cooking is a lot of work. In London or New York or any other place at sea level, it takes 3 or 4 minutes to make a soft-boiled egg. But at the top of Pikes Peak, it takes about 20 minutes. Here is the reason why.

The earth has a blanket of air all around it. This blanket is thicker at sea level than it is high up in the mountains. So air pushes down harder at sea level than it does in the mountains. We saw that water begins to boil when the molecules of water push so hard that they pop out

The earth has a blanket of air all around it

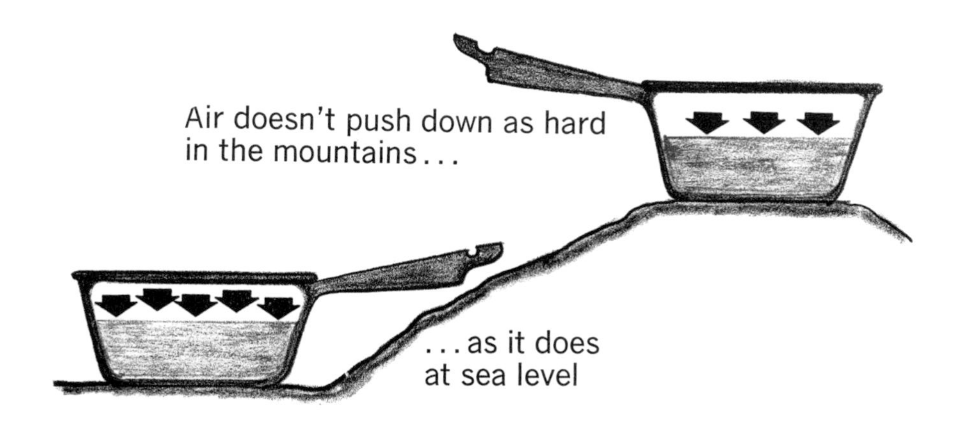

into the air as steam. The molecules will have to push harder at sea level than they do in the mountains. They will have to move faster to push back harder. They can move faster if the water gets hotter. So, at sea level, water has to get hotter before it begins to boil.

Once water is boiling, it doesn't get hotter any more. The temperature at which water boils is the hottest the water ever gets. So boiling water at sea level is hotter than boiling water in the mountains.

When an egg is cooked in boiling water, heat flows from the water into the egg. If the water is hotter, the heat flows faster. Boiling water in the mountains isn't as hot as boiling water at sea level. So an egg cooking at the top of Pikes Peak gets it heat more slowly than an egg cooking at sea level. That is why it takes longer to boil an egg at the top of Pikes Peak than at sea level.

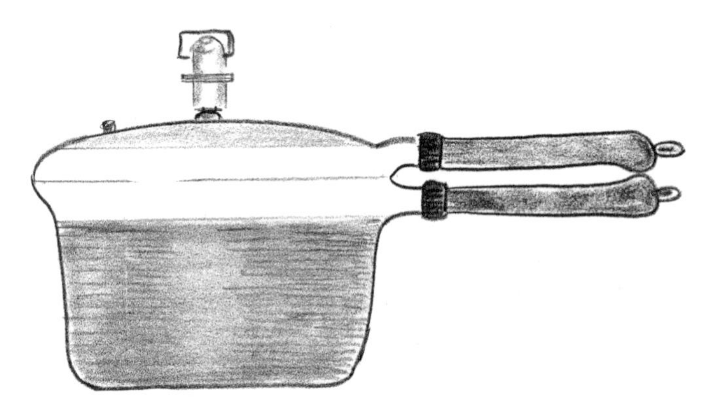

A pressure cooker

Why does it take less time to cook in a pressure cooker?

It takes about 15 minutes to cook carrots in an open pot at sea level. In a pressure cooker it takes 3 or 4 minutes. Here is the reason why.

Carrots are cooked by boiling them in water. The heat of the boiling water flows into the carrots and makes them soft. The carrots will cook faster if the water is hotter. Water that is boiling in a pressure cooker can be made hotter than water boiling in an open pot. So the carrots cook faster in a pressure cooker.

Here is how a pressure cooker works. A pressure cooker is made of a very strong metal. It has a lid that fits very tightly. The carrots and a little bit of water are put into the cooker. The lid is put on. The lid is so tight that no air can get in or out. Then the pressure cooker is put on the stove.

The heat of the stove makes the water in the pressure cooker begin to boil. The water begins to change to steam. But the lid of the cooker is very tight. So the steam can't get out of the cooker. It is in a trap. The steam mixes with the air that is in the cooker. The air pushes down on the water in the cooker. The steam also pushes down on the water in the cooker. So there is an extra hard push on the water. This push tries to keep molecules from jumping out of the water. The molecules have to move faster to jump out and keep the water boiling. The water has to get hotter for the molecules to move faster. So water is hotter when it boils in a pressure cooker. If the water is hotter, heat flows into the carrots faster. So carrots cooking in a pressure cooker get their heat more quickly than carrots cooking in an open pot. That is why it takes less time to cook in a pressure cooker than in an open pot.

Inside a pressure cooker

Why does gasoline burn but water does not?

Do you think that water doesn't burn because it is wet? Gasoline is wet, too, but it burns. To find out the reason why water doesn't burn, we first have to find out what happens when things burn.

The air around us is made up of gases. One of the gases in air is oxygen. When things burn, they use the oxygen in the air. Oxygen makes a wood fire burn. Oxygen comes together with *chemicals* (KEM-i-kals) in the wood to make other chemicals. Burning uses up the wood *and* some of the oxygen in the air. When wood is all burned, the fire goes out.

Water can't burn because it is already burned. It is

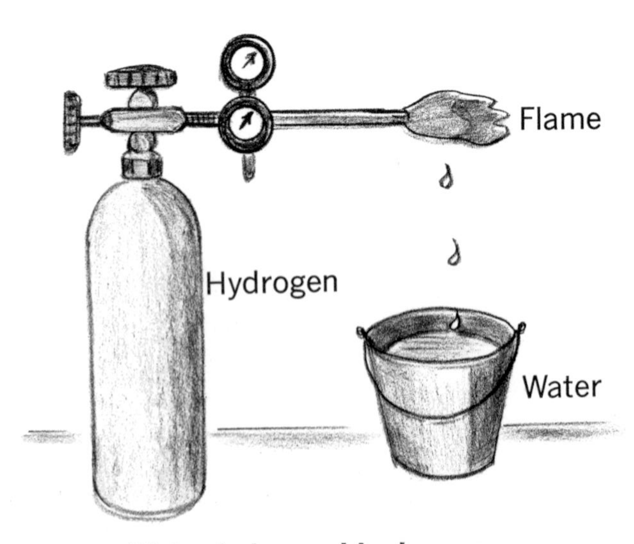

Water is burned hydrogen

made when hydrogen burns in air. Hydrogen comes together with some of the oxygen in the air to make water.

Gasoline can burn because it has chemicals in it that can come together with the oxygen in the air. Gasoline has hydrogen in it. The hydrogen in the gasoline burns to make water. Gasoline also has *carbon* (CAR-bun) in it. The carbon in it burns to make a gas called *carbon dioxide* (CAR-bun dy-OX-ide).

Because water can't burn we use it for putting some fires out. We can put out a wood fire by pouring water on it. The water keeps the wood from getting oxygen from the air. The wood cannot keep burning without oxygen.

An automobile engine makes use of the fact that gasoline burns. When the gasoline burns inside the engine, it makes the automobile run.

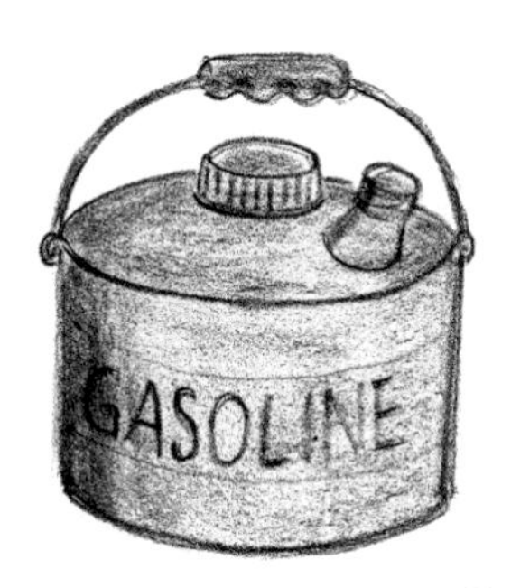

Carbon and hydrogen
in the gasoline
burn in air

Gasoline can burn

WORD LIST

Cold-blooded animal — An animal whose body temperature changes with the temperature of its surroundings.

Graphite (GRAF-ite) — A very soft mineral. You write with the graphite in a pencil.

Helium (HEE-lee-um) — A gas that is lighter than air. It does not burn.

Hydrogen (HY-dro-jen) — The lightest gas there is. It burns easily.

Molecule (MOLL-eh-kule) — The tiniest bit of anything.

Oxygen (OX-i-jen) — The gas in the air that is used up when things burn.

Paraffin (PAR-a-fin) — The stuff out of which ordinary candles are made. It burns easily.

Pressure cooker — A special pot for cooking more quickly.

Pupil — The dark opening in the eye that lets light in.

Retina (RET-in-a) — The part of the eye on which light shines after it passes through the pupil.

Saliva (sa-LIE-va) — Spit. It is made by glands in the mouth. It makes the food in your mouth wet.

Steam (steem) — The gas that is made by boiling water.

Surface (SIR-fess) — The outside of something.

Warm-blooded animal — An animal whose body temperature is always the same.

Water vapor (VAY-per) — Steam.